GETTING THAT JOB

IN

DIRECT SALES

Written By

Wayne E Shillum

This Book is Dedicated

To the Many hundreds of Resumes

That I read when searching for employees

In my own Company

Especially to the ones that never made it to the Consideration Stage

and

To those who were "New to Canada"

That I Coached and Helped to Find Sales and Marketing Jobs

Through the Canadian Institute of Marketing

and

ACCES Employment of Canada

Authors Comments

Sending large numbers of the same generic documents to almost everyone, will almost always end in disappointment and will waste your time and money.

Quality not Quantity is key to getting noticed and obtaining that first interview. Too many applications are rejected at first glance and are never read because of their appearance.

Part One - Preparation:

There is a lot of work in putting together professional looking documents. They must be crafted to meet the expectations of the people who are doing the hiring for the specific job types and environments of your choice.

Part Two – The Interview

Presenting yourself in the best possible way when arranging an interview and during your face-to-face interview are the final parts of the hiring process.

By following the steps outlined in this book you will be creating a blueprint for success and you will be on your way to *"Getting That Job in Direct Sales".*

Table of Contents

INTRODUCTION

This book is written for people looking for jobs in all types of sales, and it covers from no experience to more experience than one can put into a two-page resume.

We will provide valuable tips for both those with experience and for those new to selling, who lack experience or selling skills.

We will outline the importance of learning the essential skill sets and getting as much experience in sales and related areas as possible.

Explanations Come First

Before we get into the actual document preparation, we will explain what areas will impact the cover letter, resume and references and show you how to use them to your advantage.

We will outline some very important areas to know before you have your job interview.

Our Table of Contents does a great job of outlining what we include in the whole process of getting a sales job. Use our easy Click and go-to.

We will also explain why many who **DO HAVE** the sales experience and necessary skills are being passed over every day.

The Consideration process starts with the cover letter and resume.

If you get those Two correct you will then provide references

If they are satisfactory there will be the interview

So why are so many job applicants eliminated

Before they get out of the starting gate?

As a business owner with over 40 employees, many times I had the task of wading through 100 to 150 cover letters and resumes.

Often it would be to hire only one or two people, so I can relate to the consideration process and the importance of standing out in a positive way.

Coaching Professional Sales People

For four years; as a member of The Canadian Institute of Marketing, I coached sales and marketing professionals who were new to Canada and searching for employment.

Although these applicants were very qualified, many of their cover letters and resumes were failing in their initial presentation and they were experiencing continuous eliminated without consideration.

As I coached, I most often found that their presentation documents were poorly formatted, and the information was poorly presented. It was these two areas that became the biggest reasons for their earlier rejections.

It very often was not their qualifications. It was the presentation of them. If the Presentation is poor, it will usually result in immediate elimination.

We will outline what we consider to be the best format and presentation features to create a professional looking cover letter, resume and reference package that will get the best results possible.

All cover letters, resumes and references must do a professional job of presenting the applicants credentials; if they are to succeed.

There is more emphasis on how well one markets or sells oneself to the potential employer, when they are applying for a sales or marketing position.

The reason for the added emphasis for Perfection

Is Obvious

If you cannot sell yourself properly to the prospective employer, how can the person doing the hiring expect you to market or sell their products or services to their customers?

This is a conscious thought that will play a huge role whenever your application documents are read and when you are interviewed.

The cover letter and resume are like speeches. If the openings are not interesting and do not get the readers immediate attention or the message is not clear, the application will usually be rejected by the potential employer.

Yes, Application documents are like Speeches

Your written job application documents will have the same results as a speech that is poorly organized and is given in a monotone without any enthusiasm.

The person reading your application will become confused or bored and will stop paying attention.

The cover letter and resume become the employer's first involvement with you as a job applicant. Employers are looking for the applicants that stand out above the rest in a good way, urging them to read on and find out more about that person.

For many applicants, their Journey ends

"AT FIRST GLANCE"

- Why do so many hopeful job seekers experience this?
- Why do they not even know it is happening?
- What common mistakes are being made by people every day when they submit a cover letter or resume for employment?

Often the "First Part" of the "Hiring Process"
is "Elimination" - NOT "Consideration"

When many applications are submitted for one position the employer often looks for ways to narrow the field quickly. It may seem unfair – but it happens.

The most important first step for the applicant is the presentation of what they bring to the job. The success of this first step will depend a great deal on how compelling the cover letter and resume documents are to read.

First Viewing

How the cover letter or resume look at first viewing will often determine if those applying will even reach the consideration stage. If the documents look too crowded or too difficult to read, the process could be over.

The documents will not even be read

A professionally created cover letter and resume can overcome this elimination at first glance and give the applicant the opportunity to advance to the final part of the hiring process which is the interview.

Following the appearance issue, the next area of consideration will then be one's skill sets and experience. The candidate who lacks in these areas will need to recognize their own shortfall and be willing to find ways to enhance their hiring potential.

We will outline the ways in which a person with little experience or skills in sales can improve their chances.

Summary of Introduction

The sales category is usually the largest section of jobs offered in any area where multiple job types are advertised. Often sales jobs alone represent as much as 60 percent of those jobs advertised.

Sales is also one of the few remaining job types that will allow you to start at the bottom with little or no experience or limited skills. You can then build a professional career with almost unlimited earning capabilities that will be based on your own efforts.

It is estimated that approximately 13% of all jobs in North America (1 out of every 8 jobs) is a full-time sales position.

It is also estimated that over one Trillion dollars are spent annually on sales forces; which shows the importance to the employer of finding the right sales person for the job.

Statistics also say that 55% of the people making their living in sales don't have the right skills to be successful. This means anyone that can demonstrate that they have these skills will have an advantage.

The importance of presenting your Cover Letter, Resume, and Documents in a professional manner will make the difference in your chances of being hired.

The final hurdle which is your interview, is the moment of truth and the final deciding factor.

WHY NOT DO IT RIGHT?

WHAT YOU WILL NEED TO OFFER

Selling Skills

The Basic selling skills shown below come from the key steps involved in the sales process.

Finding Customers *("Prospecting")* This is not always required for a sales position such as in retail sales. Other company types will provide leads for you as well. Prospecting is Marketing which often becomes part of the sales duties.

Basic Sales Skills Required

- **Qualifying your Prospects**: Establishing needs and finding out if there is an interest to consider your offerings
- **Overcoming the Objections**: These will occur from first contact to the very end when you have asked for the order
- **Meetings and Presentations**: Knowing how hold first meetings, information gathering meetings and how to prepare for and make successful closing presentations
- **Closing the Sale**: How to ask for the order in multiple ways to suit the occasion and understanding which close to use and why
- **Answering the Final Objections:** How to answer the many types of objections that occur after you have asked for the order

Your Choice of Employer

By choosing a company that provides quality products or services at competitive prices, you will enhance your ability to look after your customer's needs and keep them as customers.

It is also about you providing service, dedication and dependability to your clients to earn their loyalty and enjoy their repeat business.

The Job Search is a "double-sided-process"

Choose your employer wisely. Their reputation and their credibility will affect yours. Choosing the wrong company can become a dead end for you regardless of your qualifications. It can also damage your credibility with others.

In most cases to get hired

You must be able to show that you have learned and can use your skill sets to obtain the sales required by the employer.

This will be their primary consideration and you will need to demonstrate your capabilities to them in your cover letter and resume, so you can to get to the interview stage.

Good News about Selling Skills

For those job seekers without selling skills, this is fortunately the quickest and easiest hurdle to overcome. One can take the initiative to develop these areas of knowledge (skill sets) on their own.

It should therefore become a priority to acquire these selling skills as quickly as possible, so you can get started somewhere to gain the experience you need.

If you already have them, you will be in a *"preferred status"* situation already.

Any experience in selling will improve your ability to use your skill sets. Learning and mastering these skills will create a definite advantage when competing with other "new-to-sales" candidates who do not have them.

Information Sources for Selling Skills

Check out our Sales Training at

http://www.wesmarketing.com

Our training is based on the authors successful selling methods and skill sets developed and perfected over 35 years of professional selling.

Our five Part 407-page Sales Training Manual provides the necessary information to learn the skills that are needed to become successful.

Other Sources

A quick and economical source to obtain this knowledge can be found by purchasing and reading available sales training eBooks or soft cover books found online at places like Kindle. This is a great place to find a large assortment of sales ideas, techniques, tips and strategies.

Check your local book stores for information on sales and marketing. Local libraries will often provide an economical source of information to enable you to learn and master these skill sets to begin your sales career at a quicker pace.

Often there will be people or companies who offer mentoring or coaching in your local community. As well there are many sources offering sales training on-line.

Often many sales jobs will give you the opportunity to prove your worth and show your selling capabilities with your on-the-job performance.

These are great places to start perfecting your skills and to start building your experience.

For your own benefit, make sure you have acquired the basic skill sets before you apply, or you will have little success, once in the sales position.

Job Experience

The lack of sales experience is difficult to overcome. When starting out you may have no full-time job experience to show in your cover letter or resume.

If you have worked part time while in school in any kind of sales capacity, this is part of your job experience.

Getting the experience part is not as easy as obtaining skill sets. You will need to work in a sales capacity or similar activity of marketing or promotion to get it.

Your lack of job experience

This might result in your need to consider starting in a retail position, commissioned sales position or any area requiring less selling history. Here you can build your knowledge, experience and improve your selling skills.

If you have any past activities relating to the job type advertised; including hobbies, this is a key factor as they show involvement in the employer's environment.

The goal

Aim as high as you can and make the effort to secure the best job that you can. At the same time, you must also recognize; that to reach your goal when starting out, you may need to begin at the apprenticeship level to gain this experience.

This could mean starting in a position that provides on-the-job training. As you increase your history, the useful experience content for your resume will improve. You will become more valuable as an employee.

You will then create opportunities for advancement in your existing employment, or in the consideration process for a higher-level job outside of the company.

Retail

This is often a good place for someone with little sales background to start. It does not involve *"Sales Prospecting."* Finding customers or (prospecting) is one of the more difficult areas of selling to master and usually involves some marketing skills as well.

A retail business owner will usually choose a location that has good traffic or will advertise to bring customers to their establishment.

If you can demonstrate how your personality and people skills will benefit the company and get sales for it; you will have met a major consideration of the retail owner. Any sales training will move you closer to a prime consideration spot.

Commission Sales

Often a position of commissioned sales is another good area to start. Many jobs of this type will include training of the skill sets needed for selling. The biggest obstacle here could be staying power without a salaried income.

Other Experience

Showing anything relating to working with people will be beneficial for your *"other experience"* part of your resume.

Sales is developing and using your people skills, and this is a very important part of servicing your clients effectively.

Showing any activity; whether it is involvement in a drama club, sports team, membership in a local organization or a charity will demonstrate that you are people oriented.

Academic Qualifications

For Sales

There are now some universities and colleges that will offer courses in sales and sales management where you will get a degree or certificate upon successful course completion.

This proof of training will enhance your cover letter and resume but will often involve taking "on-campus" courses and paying some sizable dollars.

A Business Administration degree in Marketing can also be an asset for sales as many sales jobs do involve some form of marketing. However; often there is very little, if anything, dedicated to actual sales training included in a marketing course.

Usually the higher level of professional sales or sales management jobs will see these types of degrees as a plus for qualifications and consideration for a position.

Special knowledge

A specialized degree is often required by employers who have products or services relating to niche markets or a specialized field. In these cases, there will be little chance of being hired if one does not have the academic qualifications.

The employer will rely on this educational requirement to establish if applicants have a basic knowledge of their business subject matter (products or services) and can speak effectively and with authority to their clients.

These scholastic requirements will automatically reduce the number of people applying and the number of those to be considered.

Sales experience here is a big asset

Often people with these academic qualifications will have little or no in-the-field sales experience. If one has this academic training and can show any actual part time or full-time sales experience it should be stated in the cover letter or resume.

Any Involvement servicing the public is an asset

It will put that person into a better candidate status for an interview.

Sales experience and having the skill sets will be what every potential employer is after when looking for a sales representative. Lack of these components is what every candidate will need to overcome.

References

Your references should be specific to the job in question. You should be able to draw on a pool of possible references to suit the job in question. Too many job applicants will use the same references for every application and that is a recipe for disaster.

There are two types of references that one will consider for any application. One will be a character reference and the other will relate to your experience for the job type being offered.

You should learn which type or if both will benefit your cause. Using the wrong type will not impress the person reviewing them. We will discuss references further in the following chapters.

Interviews

Your interview is the final step in the job search process and if you make it this far it will become your best opportunity to complete that journey. Do not ever assume that you have it made, if you reach the interview stage.

There are many ways to destroy everything you have achieved up to this point. It is the final and pivotal point that offers the best opportunity to communicate the reasons why the potential employer should choose you for the position.

Overview Summary

You need to get your foot in the door and get started on the experience journey. This could mean showing a willingness to learn and an eagerness to prove yourself by starting at whatever level you can.

The cover letter and resume content will change with your increased education and experience. These documents will demonstrate the level of professionalism that you have reached.

The higher that the required level of professionalism is; the higher will be the demand for the effective presentation of your experience, training and skills in your submitted documents.

Leveraging

Use the experience from your first jobs to keep leveraging your way to better positions within a company or outside of it as the opportunities arise.

Stay long enough in these positions to show stability and that you have had time to learn. A history of frequent job changing does not look good on any resume.

Make the effort to start as high as you can but make sure you can do what is required in the position you seek.

The expression *"Biting off more than you can chew"*

Did not come about without cause

If the results of your job searches reveal that you are aiming too high to get started, perhaps it would be a practical decision to start where you can.

In this way you can start getting the job history that you will need for the better jobs and allow you to fine tune your skills.

Unless you can get started and obtain the experience first (that the higher paying jobs will require), you will always be on the outside looking in.

You will get caught in

The Revolving Door

"You need Experience to get the Job

And a Job to get the Experience"

TIPS AND STRATEGIES

The Employers Qualifications

If you qualify for a job at any level, it is important for you to make the right decision of where you will seek employment.

Many people do not give enough thought in choosing a company with a good reputation, image and quality products. Take the time to research your choices to find a company or companies that have these traits before you make your final selection(s) to pursue a job opportunity.

This can pay many times over in the level of your own success.

Products and Services

What is equally important as choosing the right company is making sure their products or services fulfill a need and can provide tangible benefits to the customer!

These beneficial features will complete the three most important ingredients of your sales employment package

1. *Income Potential*
2. *Company Image*
3. *Quality Offerings*

A good company image and quality offerings *(products or services)* presented to your prospects will determine your income potential.

You may be looking at several job opportunities; therefore, doing your proper research up front will make sure that you will start in the right direction for a successful career.

Companies Chosen

Once you have found the company or companies to which you wish to apply, follow these important steps so that you have the best chance possible to get the position when you present your cover letter, resume and references.

One should do enough research to gain a good basic knowledge of the company, its product(s) or service(s)?

- When did it start, who started it, and who is running it now?
- What features make them a good company to work for?
- Do they have a good reputation?
- Do they have happy employees?
- What are their products and/or services? – "all of them"
- Are their products/services quality or just at the acceptable level?
- Do their products/services have real benefits?
- Who are their main competitors and where are their products positioned for quality and price when compared to the company you are considering?
  - This is important because they will become your competition when hired.

Consider all this information when preparing your cover letter and resume and if possible, use references that have a similar background to the companies you are applying to.

Comfort Zone

The above suggestions are going to give you a comfort level of knowledge about the company.

Do not go overboard. Getting all the information is not essential. You will substantially increase the consideration for the job if you can show that you have a basic knowledge of these areas.

Just do your best when gathering it without becoming overly visible by calling the potential employer too many times. Use the internet or local directories for information as much as you can.

Things you should know about Commissions

You should know this before you accept a job. Often there will be a job description where you might find this information. If not available in the job description, the interview is the place to learn these things.

Sometimes the way of calculating commission can be quite complex and it is best to make sure you fully understand what your sales targets are, and how you will be paid.

Examples

- Is your commission based on all sales or is there a level you must reach to justify your salary first, and commissions begin thereafter?
- Will your commission be calculated on everything or just everything over that base?
- Are all commissions at the same rate or is there any kind of graduating scale based on different types of products or different levels in sales volume?
- If your sales are for projects that have progress payments find out:
    - If you get paid for the entire sale up front when the sale is made
    - As the customer is invoiced
    - As the payments come in
- How soon after the above conditions are met are commissions paid?
- What happens if there is nonpayment or a hold back by the customer for a reason caused by someone else in your company? Do you still get your commission?

The following subject is often never addressed until it is too late; but it can become very costly to you, if it is not addressed at some point in the hiring process.

Find out what happens to your Commissions?

- If you have a lot of long term contracts or projects in the works, and you are laid off or terminated. Do you still get paid for these sales already made?

- If you have a large blanket order or an annual contract. Do you receive commissions to the end of the contract or for any length of time after you are laid off or terminated?

- If you are laid off or terminated. What are the conditions of termination that will negate any commissions or bonuses owing?

Try to get this information established clearly and put into your sales agreement. If they will not do this, consider looking elsewhere.

It is amazing how some employers forget about your hard work, your reputation or the relationship with the customer and the trust that you have built, when they are faced with the payment of a large commission that you have earned.

Avoiding Payment

Firing to avoid paying large commissions does occur occasionally and could result in your loss of large amounts of income.

I know it happens because I found out the hard way and lost some very large commissions for that very reason.

Having a clause in your sales agreement to outline how this situation is handled is important but it should be addresses very carefully.

Is there some kind of protection for you? Perhaps include a clause outlining reasons for justifiable termination. If the termination is not justified what happens to the outstanding commissions.

It could be that all commissions are due and payable immediately, if proper procedures are not followed for dismissal or there is no justifiable cause?

Remember these words

What has Not Been Written

Has Never Been Said!

Get everything in writing in the beginning, so there are no questions. Discuss these points immediately prior to you officially being hired, or when you are hired before sales agreements or contracts are finalized.

Today even though sales people are protected by wrongful dismissal legislation, it is still best to avoid a situation like this, if you can.

Consider your Sales contract as your - *"Sales Prenuptial*

Payment of commissions can become a grey area very quickly – especially if you are terminated and the amounts owing are large.

AGAIN: Handle this very carefully. The wrong approach could create bad results and no job.

Reputable companies will usually not object to clarity in how you are paid and will spell it out in writing as part of your employment agreement with them.

Beware of those who will not put things in writing!

Expenses

If they are paid, make sure you know how and when.

- Immediately upon submission
- Within 3 – 5 days of submission (week days or calendar days)
- Upon a certain date

Advances on Commission

- Are they paid at all?
- Is there any kind of advance when you start?
- Do you need sales or commissions earned to get an advance?
- How much or what percentage can you get against sales made?
- Is there an overall limit?
- What is expected with advances if you are terminated?

What happens with customer hold backs (nonpayment for any reason)? Do they affect your commission or bonus? They really should not unless you caused the hold back.

Social Media

Social media has added value for the all applicants as they enter the job search market. Having your own large audience in social media can now be considered a potential game changer for those with less sales experience giving them added value.

The typical social media participant may have a base of 130 to 160 of what we will call contacts on one networking site.

Examples

It could be Face book, Twitter, LinkedIn, or any of the many others available. Some statistics will say that there is an average extended level of one's potential contact base of 20,000 plus for each social network with these 130 to 160 first level contacts.

This extended number is based on extensions created by likes, comments and sharing at optimum levels. This will be considered an asset for many employers.

Someone with 300 - 400 contacts or more for each of 2 or 3 social sites could be considered a very valuable addition to a company, if the applicants contacts are potentials for the companies target market.

If your social networking activity involves the type of product or service that a business you are applying to is involved in; this can help your chances considerably, so make sure you mention it.

Having a large social media presence is considered very valuable and often provides the newer, less experienced recruit; with some preferred status. Do not underestimate the importance of this asset in your cover letters or resumes.

Warning: Make sure it is clearly understood that these contacts remain yours and do not become property of your employer. Some may try; but, you should not be required to provide these contacts as part of your employment.

You should never be requested or expected to provide any information or passwords to the potential employer, no matter how badly you want the position or how much they say that they want you for it.

AREAS TO CONSIDER

As good as the sales profession can be, it is important to know its dark side to avoid making the mistakes that can make your success very difficult or even impossible.

Protect All of Your Contacts

If you have been in the industry for some time and have built up a list of contacts, this is a great asset. Do not provide this information before you start working for the company.

Make sure you clearly establish the fact that your lists of friends, followers and contacts that you bring with you and new ones you develop will remain your own assets, should you be terminated.

They are Your Lists

You may inform your contacts on your own volition of your new position and make mention of the products or services as well as inform them of any product or service promotions that your employer is making.

In the larger scope of things most companies fortunately are ethical and the examples that we have just provided are meant as cautionary. Sales can become a very rewarding career and the good employers far outweigh the bad.

Non-Compete Clauses

Be very careful when faced with this situation. You should always be able to keep the contacts that you bring with you or new ones that you obtain, if you leave on your own or if you are fired.

Non-Compete clauses should be voided if you are laid off or fired.

If not handled properly you could find yourself starting all over again in a new industry or market without being able to use your contacts.

Unethical Operators

If your employer has no regard for the customer or their needs, you are choosing the wrong company and it will become a dead-end job. Get ready to move on when your conscience catches up to you, or the unhappy customers do.

You might know the kind of companies I am talking about.

These are the ones where there is no real need for the product, and the whole sales structure is a multitude of high pressure-based closes, with no regard for what the customer may want or need.

Do you really want to brag about where you work, if this is the company you have chosen?

The Bottom Feeders

The following is my personal summation of how I see the bottom feeders of Sales. It stems from some of my own early experiences in several direct sales situations.

I tried many different companies and product types in my early years. These types were always very easy places to get hired.

I wasted many days and evenings in numerous job types before realizing who was winning.

It was usually not me

Their Business Model

This type of company is based on frequent ads for sales positions, hiring in mass quantities and siphoning off the residue (sales) from the group passing through at any given time.

One group of sales people has all but disintegrated just as the next one is starting. This next batch is recruited, processed and launched "just in time" to keep the sales coming in for the company.

This description is unfortunately more right than wrong, and these types of sales jobs are perhaps the most difficult environment for new sales people to survive in.

Reason for Leaving the Profession

It is probably the biggest reason why many who try this type of sales do not stay in the sales profession after their experience.

You will usually find yourself as one of many new recruits from the company's most recent search for sales people. You will be part of a large group sales training session where you will be expected to memorize a sales presentation format written by the company.

You will also be expected to provide a few "in house" product demonstrations to show that you have mastered the sales approach.

You might get cards to write your name on when you start. If you make it through the first phase and get some sales, you might even get some cards printed for you at the employer's expense; but the printed ones are usually hard to get.

Many of these companies will supply a sales kit that you will sign for and must return on departure.

The cost of the kit will usually be withheld from your first pay if not paid for up front. Most will ask for a deposit up front for a kit because they know you may quit and not bring it back.

They will return the deposit if you return the kit when you leave. They will usually write off the cards.

How They Operate

Leads most often are supplied by the company with a small percentage of the commission going to the telemarketer or person obtaining the lead.

These leads are often obtained under questionable expectations from the prospect who often is not quite certain why you are there.

The prospect often thinks that the sales person is delivering a gift. In return they will watch a "no obligation" demonstration of a new product and offer their opinion of it.

Often the product is not new, or it has not even been revealed to the client, by the telemarketer. At best it is vaguely referenced or often given a pseudonym.

Expenses

It is rare that any expenses are covered by this type of employer and the sales representative will usually pay for all travel. One will usually be an "Independent Sales Person".

This means looking after all expenses and deductions.

Have a thick skin and be prepared for many doors not answered, door closings, prospects not in, appointments suddenly too busy to see you or examples of just plain rudeness.

Your Application requirements for this type of Sales will almost never require a cover letter or resume.

An application may be filled out when you show up, but will be for appearances or record keeping, in case you should remain for any time.

The Interview is often very quick to see if you have a tax number for deductions and a means of transportation to reach the potential customers.

Most often there will be no one-on-one interview and in its place, there will be a group presentation by the company that is made to everyone showing up.

All the application requirements are mostly fulfilled by just showing up and watching their presentation.

The presentation is usually followed by a short break to get rid of the faint-of-heart. The first break often will see 50% - 60% or more of the people leave. It is usually more gradual after the first exodus, but it is continuous.

The Myths

There is always mention of the huge amounts of dollars that other sales people are making. Often the amounts are so high that you would be happy with half or even one third of the amounts.

At best those people are very few and you may never actually see or meet them. You will almost never get real proof of these claims.

The one thought to keep in mind

"If it sounds too good to be true, it usually is"

The Legends

You are often trained by managers who used to be ordinary sales people like you will be. They have reportedly risen through the ranks to become senior management.

This is meant to show you where your future could lead, and these types of companies will almost always produce these legends during the first session.

Remember

The reputation that you build in the beginning of your career, maintain and build upon during the life of it; will become your greatest ally, or your greatest enemy.

The choice is up to you!

THE COVER LETTER

COVER LETTER TIPS

Your cover letter is your introduction to the prospective employer. It is like reading the preface of a book to see if they might be interested in reading further.

The cover letter should be very specific to the job in question. One Cover letter does not fit all job opportunities. Many applicants will make this mistake by generalizing too much.

Saving time in this manner will result in a great deal of wasted time that you will generate later by your extended job search.

Writing Your Cover Letters

We say cover letters (plural) because your cover letter should be written to specifically suit the company and position for which you are applying. If there are five job types that you are applying for; then there should be five different cover letters – one to suit each job type.

It must be a true fit – not one type fits all.

This is where you bring out specifics that match the position and requirements where you are applying, showing your experiences and successes that will demonstrate why you are suited for the job.

The cover letter is your initial introduction to the company and many job applicants overlook the importance of the cover letter altogether.

By including a cover letter and by doing it well you can obtain a definite advantage. Cover letters are often used by the employer to eliminate candidates, without even seeing the resume.

This can happen especially if there are many applicants for the position. If you do not have a cover letter, you could simply be passed over because it will show lack of effort.

Information You Need

When applying for an advertised job you will most times be supplied with all the important information for your reply.

If information is lacking or you are doing your own searches and applying for jobs not advertised on job boards or in other listings. You can find most of the following information on the internet or in any up to date local directory or the library.

- Get the company's correct name
- Management infra-structure (Their who's who)
- Products and services
- Main competition if possible
- Address and telephone number
- Call and ask who would look after hiring for your job type, if you are doing your own job search
  - Get the person's name, correct spelling of it and their title.
  - Get their telephone number or extension for future follow up.

Often it may take a second or third call to collect all necessary information.

Blind Addressing

Avoid sending blind letters – To *Hiring Manager* – unless they are part of instructions in a job position advertised. Even then a name along with the title is best if you can get it.

For cold job searching or blanket applications *"Blind References"* often do not reach their proper destination as no job has been advertised.

A letter sent without a name can be opened or discarded by anyone and never be missed.

They also look very *"Unprofessional"* as well.

Always follow up by telephone where possible as it adds 38% more success potential to your efforts. Keep copies of each cover letter for follow up.

Keep Your Correspondence Formal

One big mistake to avoid is becoming too familiar when addressing your letters or replies. Do not use first name like *Dear Bill or Dear Cathy*.

You will usually upset or anger the person responsible because this shows little respect for authority. Your document could go straight to the waste bin.

COVER LETTER CONTENT

From the beginner to the top professional level, a cover letter can say things that the resume cannot because resumes are more structured. The Cover Letter is your personal introduction to the employer.

If you are a person with experience you will have a great deal more to say here regarding experience.

New to Sales

If you have little or no sales experience, your chances are still good. The answer is to come up with a positive statement. The way to handle this situation is to write about the characteristics and skills you do have.

You might write something like: *"I fully understand that experience is always an important part of the consideration process when you are looking to hire someone.*

Although I have no full-time history, my part time jobs as sales clerks while going to school provided a great amount sales experience."

Briefly reference the work place examples that you have presented in your resume

With Sales Experience

If you have any amount of experience in Selling, your cover letter should match the type of job you are applying for with related information pointing out where this experience will be a benefit to the employer.

If not, an identical match you can show related duties or refer to the client base if they are at all similar.

For someone with sales experience, it is even more important not to make one cover letter suit all applications.

If a potential employer views a generic one-suits-all cover letter it shows laziness and someone that cuts corners.

It is a good indication of what they can expect from that person and your opportunity for employment is lost.

Experience gives the opportunity to show similarities in job types to the one being applied for; so, show them, or keep looking.

Other Important Areas

Say why you have applied. If it is Retail and a pet store, you can point out how much you like pets. If you have pets or have been around them or looked after them, make it a key component in your cover letter.

If it is a sports store where you are applying for a position, point out your interests or involvement in sports as a participant and/or as a spectator.

Maybe you have a hobby such as plants or gardening. This also can be used if applying for a position in a gardening supply outlet or any related sales position.

Your Goals

- Point out key factors that they will be looking for in the position
- You love the challenge of Retail, order desk,

  Commission sales or whatever you have chosen
- You like working with people.
- You like pets, sports, plants, shoes, welding, chemistry
- The hours are perfect, and the location is great.
- Use anything that fits.
- You have heard good things about their products or services

Vary your approach to suit the type of sales job that you are interested in.

Examples for a sales job in Sporting equipment inside or outside sales

1. *I was an avid participant in all sports activities in school. I presently belong to summer baseball and soccer leagues with many connections. My knowledge and contacts could be a benefit for your company.*

2. *I am involved in both hockey and curling leagues in my community. My participation in advertising and sales promotions for them will benefit your company if hired.*

3. *Selling for your sports company would allow you to benefit from my past involvement in sports and from my sales training.*

4. *My passion for sports, as well as my connections in all the organizations and social media groups that I am part of (shown in my resume) will be a great benefit for your company.*

Note: Always say how your experience will benefit the employer.

Create Enthusiasm

There is nothing worse than a dry monologue in written form. Use words that show enthusiasm or excitement. Do not overdo it as a little enthusiasm goes a long way.

- Use words that create strong emotions
- Use your thesaurus for sourcing and to avoid being repetitive
- Utilize your dictionary to prevent using the wrong words or misspelling them.

Show Your Desire to Learn

Someone who demonstrates enthusiasm and a willingness to learn will often be selected over a *"know-it-all"* with more experience.

The employer knows that these types of people who *"know it all"* can be hard to handle or train.

Location and Transportation

If it is an inside position and you are located close by, make this a key point to benefit the employer for job attendance. If it is close enough for you to walk it is even better.

Having a reliable vehicle can be a very important part of the hiring process. It is especially true if the distance for you to travel is a little further from the business location or it in not easily accessible by public transportation.

On-the-Road-Sales

It will usually be an essential part of the requirements to have your own transportation for this position.

Point out the fact that you have a reliable vehicle and state year and model if it is so. This information will help in the final consideration process.

Other Training

Mention any sales or motivational training you have taken. "I have taken these sales courses and seminars (whatever you have done). I have prepared myself, to be able to prospect, make presentations, and close the sale and to answer objections." Name your source.

All that you can do when you have little or no job experience is to build on your training or other similar experiences. Keep looking and you and eventually you will get someone's attention.

Of course, experience provides one with a larger source of examples for your cover letter. Still be selective and choose the best examples for the job you are applying for.

Mention "ANY" Experience working with People

That Might Show you have People Skills

Experience Worth Mentioning

- o A summer job in a hardware store
- o Working part time driving for a drug store while in school
- o You have directed many plays for a local drama club.
- o You were a Campaign manager for someone running for school president.
- o You held a summer job as a counselor at a resort.

Be positive and show why this experience will benefit the employer

The Cover Letter Ending

If you have little or no sales experience, your chances are not great especially in the more professional levels.

The only way to handle this situation is to write about it in a positive way. Talk about the characteristics and skills you do have. Put your version of the following in your cover letter ending not the body of your resume.

This concept will also work

For the Experienced person as well

"You are looking for a person who has the desire and enthusiasm to successfully present your products/services to your clients and get sales.

Granting me an interview will allow you to discover that I am the right person to do the job. I look forward to meeting with you and will call to arrange a time."

The most important part of your cover letter ending

Is to ask for an interview.

Whether you are new to sales or an experienced sales candidate this demonstrates a very important part of the sales process and that is asking for the order or the interview.

Summary

- Keep your cover letter reference and topic specific to the job applied for and do not use a generic type that will suit many job categories.
- Keep your letter simple and show what they ask for is what you offer.
- Always ask for an interview and finish on a positive note.

We have provided a lot of suggestions in this chapter to people new to sales as they will usually have the most difficulty in getting started.

Experience will give the candidate more options and opportunities.

THE RESUME

WRITTEN CONTENT

Your resume is not a biography. It is more informative than your cover letter and should be focused on the job you are applying for. There are many mistakes made when writing a resume and we will cover most of them in the next chapter. *"The Mistakes People Make"*

Resumes are meant to create or enable the interview. If you try to tell it all in the resume there may be little or no desire for the prospective employer to meet with you and discuss the possibilities of your employment.

We say Resumes (plural)

The same concept of being specific applies here as it does in your cover letter, but a resume is a little more generic than the cover letter.

The resume can be written to reach a little larger audience and can show a wider range of experiences whereas the cover letter is very specific.

However; you should have a separate resume theme for each main type of job that you may be applying for. Make any changes when applying to suit the potential employer in question.

One resume does not suit all jobs or categories as many people think.

Take time to do it right

Should be your motto

Example: - You might have experience in all the following areas; therefore, you could have a different resume for each.

When applying to any one of these company types or other types, match your experience with them.

You will place emphasis on the appropriate job history.

Examples

- Retail sales selling electronic equipment.
- Industrial supplies - on the road selling to manufacturing.
- Commercial Leasing - leasing office space or retail space.

Why are they different

- Each one will probably have different customer demographics and advertising methods to reach the prospects.
- Your customer needs for Industrial supplies may not be very useful for leasing.
- Retail sales experience does not involve prospecting or finding your own clients.

Your results will be reflected by your efforts - so keep asking yourself what type of results do I want? Do I want Poor, Average or Great?

Resume Appearance

As mentioned earlier from my own hiring experience; the decision to read further or to eliminate for most resumes is often made at first glance.

This fact is echoed by many of my peers who do a lot of hiring

Layout, spacing, font size and clarity are key factors and they can be as important as the resume content itself; perhaps even more important.

If it looks too difficult to read, it will usually not be read, and your qualifications will not matter.

Too many people try to say it all in their resume and crowd everything together to say it. They use smaller font size and eliminate much needed spacing.

The well know phrase **"Less is More"** should be remembered here as well.

Presentation Tips

Your Presentation of your resume is especially important because you will often be preparing quotations and presentations for the employer. These skills become extremely visible here.

The more professional the position is that you seek, the more important that these factors will be. They are always important and will never be lost at any level of job that you are seeking.

Effectively demonstrating them to your prospective employer, will always place you higher on the list for consideration.

Because one resume does not suit all job types, you must build your resume to suit the job category you are after. Make your experience and job history reflects benefits for the job in question.

Make as many experience references as you can to the actual job that you are applying for, so that your resume does not appear generic and is used for every job that you are seeking.

Job Experience

As you move up in the sales profession, having knowledge and experience in the job type is a key factor. If you do not have a lot of experience mention things like you have read a lot about or researched the job type.

If you know good points about the business mention this but do not over do this part. Show the knowledge that you have of their company and their products or services.

The higher the level that you are considering in the sales profession, the more important the following skill sets will become.

1. How to stay positive and show that you possess the key selling traits
2. How to Prospect – multiple ways
3. How to effectively gather information for your quotations
4. How to make Presentations, hold meetings, do demonstrations
5. How to Close a Sale – knowledge of at least 10 or more closes and your understanding of how and where to use them in the sales process

6.   How to Overcome Objections – Answer them and get the sale.

These skill sets will be very helpful and powerfully increase your chances of getting any sales position. They form the basics of selling, and they are the most important components to show in both your cover letter and resume.

Social Media

If you have a good or large following on Face book, Twitter, LinkedIn or a group related to the job, those connections can be considered an asset so make sure you mention them.

The larger the following - the greater your potential value, when you say: *"I now work at X company and they have great products and services. Come in and see me"* or *"Check out our website"* or *"Can we get together?"*

These connections (if you have them) could help the owner obtain higher traffic a potentially greater sales numbers. They will be high on the list of desired traits that they will look for in the person to be hired.

Show your number of social media connections and contacts if they are reasonably high. If your numbers are low, leave the quantity blank as low numbers may have the opposite effect.

Education

Academic credentials are always important and if they are relevant for the position, provide the information to show that you have achieved them.

If you have letters to show such as MBA or others; show them. They do make a difference.

Always name where you obtained your degree or accreditation and when. If you leave this information out they may question the validity.

Key Groups and Organizations

Sales is a social occupation and having exposure by participating in any organization is good. List them and show your activity.

Your resume should be streamlined to suit the type of business that you are applying to. Focus on any organizations you may have joined during your education process or following it where you played any part in sales, promotions or advertising.

More examples

If you are now part of any other group(s) where you can demonstrate an involvement in sales or marketing, use it. Create similarities in these experiences to the job you are applying to.

If you are not presently part of any organizations, consider joining as many as you can handle and get involved wherever you can with their sales, promotions, and advertising.

Try to find a common thread of experience, interests or hobbies that you have, and link them to the job that you are applying for.

Marketing Skills

Often marketing can be part of a sales position, so point out any events you may have helped organize or you provided the advertising for. Talk about how successful they were.

Maybe you helped organize and promote a walk to raise money for feeding the hungry or sending aid to flood victims.

Summary

As a person just starting out, you have a lot to learn so do not hide it. Show your desire to tackle new things and desire to learn.

Write about it emphasizing the skills and knowledge that you do have.

Maybe you learned how to create and implement your own web site, so say it.

You will need to show that you have the transportation means to provide good attendance and can show up on time and be dependable.

For those who have the experience and skill sets, it will be a little easier to qualify and once again do not become generic. Show how your experience and skill sets will benefit the employer.

THE BIGGEST MISTAKES

Creating the First Impression

When I critique cover letters and resumes during my coaching, it is the first impression created by them that is my initial concern.

The appearance of the Cover Letter or Resume will usually say it all. It is here that the decision whether to continue and to read it; or to discard it, is often made by the employer.

Appearance creates the first impression and it can become your greatest reason for being considered, or not being considered.

Verbosity

It does not matter what level of job one is seeking, another big and very frequent mistake made by resume writers is that they try to say too much and crowd too much into a small space.

I say small space because a cover letter should be one page and a resume should be two pages.

It seems that the more experience that one has obtained and the higher the level of formal education that one has achieved, increases the danger of saying too much.

The remedy to this overcrowding is not achieved by increasing the number of pages, reducing the amount of open space or reducing the font size.

A secret to *"CONTENT"*

Comes from the comedy segment of show biz

The saying is - *"Leave them Laughing"*

Leave them excited and wanting more should always be the plan. Do not tell a life story and bore the reader with too much detail.

Spacing and Length

Often the page is one big mass of words with little or no spacing with long sentences joined by multiple ands, along with other conjunctions. It also has many types of emphasis used and because of all these things, the reader/employer is not likely to even attempt to read it.

Many resume writers are guilty of this syndrome

Exaggerated example - Common Mistakes

<u>**You have only two pages**</u> for your resume and you have too much to say and you now reduce the font size to 8 and sacrifice spacing by crowding everything into one large paragraph with **no breathing room** and you create <u>**emphasis for your titles**</u> with bold and even underline them and your sentences are long and you use the *and* conjunction and others to get things said and your messages become combined with others. <u>**You feel**</u> that your you have now been able to cover everything you wanted to say and can still squeeze it into the two pages that meet the required criteria and now the <u>**potential reader**</u> has all of the information that you wanted to provide with all of the duties and accomplishments from your part time jobs and your full time jobs <u>over the last five years</u> and you have even been able to provide **full detains** on your successes in school. **Your part time jobs** could cover five or six and possibly even more and by the time you make a list of your duties and achievement for all these the reader's head is spinning and they will stop that is if they started **in the first place.**

Who really wants to tackle reading the paragraph above?

How about seeing two pages of it in a resume?

(Same goes for the 1-page cover letter)

Elimination not Consideration

This unfortunately is very often the first part of the hiring process. The higher that the number of applicants for the position is, the higher will be the reasons for automatic rejections.

You did your cover letter the right way and the reader is now looking at your resume. You can be eliminated at first glance here as well.

Most Often

These discarded resumes will not ever be read. Many discarded resumes could have higher qualifications and be better applicants than the ones remaining for consideration.

Make sure your cover letters and resumes are easy to read. Make sure your messages are clear.

The cover letter is your introduction, your first encounter and is the wetting of the appetite of YOU. Your resume is step two and must clearly outline your qualifications.

If both are presented correctly, the employer will want to know more about YOU and will continue reading and call you for an interview.

If you avoid the mistakes often made; as discussed in the next Chapter as well, you will have a very good chance of being considered for an Interview.

OTHER MISTAKES

Messaging

Multiple Messages

Often, I find that in this crowded jungle of never ending words (that some people call a cover letter or resume); each sentence will have three or more topics.

In this mixed communication, any intended message can be totally lost along with your chances for consideration. Keep your messages clear and simple to understand.

Too Many Examples

When providing examples in a cover letter or resume often people go overboard to prove their capability or success in that area. Usually one or two examples are enough per job history category.

I have seen as many as 10 or more examples of Duties or Accomplishments per job description. Often similar duties or accomplishments are shown in other jobs of the same resume as well. This is what is called *"OVERKILL"*.

One or two duties, and one or two accomplishments per job with no duplications in other areas is the best possible way to present these examples.

Point Form should be just that!

Use short focused points of 1 to 2 lines for each point - 2 ½ to 3 lines per point tops.

- Many people feel that *Point Form* is just something with bullets, numbers, letters or dashes in front.
- Their points end up being 5 or 6 lines - sometimes even more.
- There are often 3 or more messages per point. (not point form)

Do not overuse any one type of point form as it will become overwhelming (Especially with bullets like in this section).

- Break it up or change the appearance where it makes sense.
    - Perhaps further indent some points which can change appearance.
    - Bullets seem to be the most intrusive; whereas, dashes quietly make the same point.
- Keep in mind that changing point type **too many times** can also be distracting and annoying.
- When finished – step back and examine the appearance. Be objective. If it does not look right change it.

Abbreviations

Unless they are extremely common like AM or PM; there is only one reason to use Abbreviations, and that is to save space if they are being used more than once.

They must be written long form first followed immediately by the abbreviated version in brackets before using the abbreviation again. Abbreviation first followed by the long form in brackets is also acceptable.

The Mistake

Do not use the abbreviation without the long form to explain what it means. You might know what the abbreviation means but the reader may not.

Many times, Abbreviated letters can have multiple meanings and used solely on their own will create misunderstanding. Used without the full versions explanation invites uncertainty.

As soon as you create uncertainty or vagueness, you enable loss of interest and lower or lose your chances for consideration.

Example – CPG

You are applying for a job in a company that sells shipping supplies or a company that sells accounting software.

You say: *"My experience in CPG has provided me with extensive knowledge in this area and dealing with people."*

What is CPG?

- Church Pension Group
- Comprehensive Procurement Guidelines
- Clinical Practice Guidelines
- Center for Politics and Governance
- Consumer Packaged Goods

Take your choice because it could be any of the above or one of many others. (*The above results came from typing CPG into a google search*)

Trade Terms

Unless your resume is written specifically for someone in your trade, leave trade terms out altogether because they have no place in most resumes.

Let's say it is a company selling wood working products. You want to demonstrate your knowledge of tools.

Example you provide – *I am proficient in the use of an electrostatic gun?*

- Is it a stun gun?
- Is it something to measure amps?
- Is it something to spray paint with?
- Not everyone will know

Of course, if you are applying for a sales position selling paint application equipment, use of this description is permitted.

Reference to another Area

Often people will say something like: "*My duties here were the same as at "ABC Company*".

Who wants to go back to find out what it was that you did for *"ABC Company"*? Most people will not go back, and they become extremely annoyed or insulted by what they see as *laziness or stupidity.*

The employer does not want to hire either one of these characteristics.

Overuse of "I"

It can easily happen. You are obviously trying to impress the potential employer and show them your accomplishments. I did this. I did that. Too many uses of I can create the wrong impression – that you are not a team player.

Rephrase your sentences and eliminate the overuse of **"I"** where you can.

Remember that you will be joining their team and will need to work with everyone. Use "we" where it is appropriate as it shows teamwork. A group effort deserves group credit.

Appearance

Font Size

Often to meet the standard format of 1 page for cover letter and 2 pages for the resume, the normal font size of 12 will be reduced to 10 to squeeze it all in. I have seen it as low as 8 in some applications. Using either 8 or 10 is not an acceptable way to say more.

If you need to reduce font size

You have already said too much.

Emphasis

This is an area where people often get carried away. They want to emphasize a word or phrase and then emphasize something else that is also important. Very soon everything becomes important, so they use additional ways to achieve emphasis.

This is not acceptable in cover letters, resumes or references.

You saw an earlier example of small font, no spacing and attempts to emphasize different parts of the paragraph and what was your reaction. <u>Underlining</u> your words for emphasis, using **Bold** in the middle of a sentence to set something apart or **<u>using both</u>** only creates more confusion. Increasing font size is another mistake as it adds to the muddle. *When Italics* or color is added the resume takes on the appearance of a scrabble board.

Keep it clean in appearance. We will cover how to present your documents in our section on design criteria.

Language, Spelling and Grammar

Large Words

Unless you are applying for a position to create cross-word puzzles, leave the humungous, brainy words behind. No one wants to try and figure out what you really mean.

Clarity is one of the greatest elements that you need to have in your cover letter or resume. Without clarity any intended message is lost in a sea of words along with your hopes for consideration.

Choosing a word that does not fit what you want to really say can create confusion. A dictionary or thesaurus will help you choose the right words.

Confusion Leads to Rejection

Spelling

There is nothing worse than a misspelled word. It could be the greatest resume ever written - and then BANG! - Loss of credibility - because of incorrect spelling.

Spell check is available in most writing formats – so use it!

Even if your format has automated spell check, when you are finished click on spelling and grammar review and do a final check.

Put yourself in the Employer's Shoes

It is amazing what little things can totally ruin your chances. Look at your resume as if you were the potential employer.

- Does it look organized?
- Does it get immediate attention?
- Would you read it? Is it Likeable?
- Are the opening statements clear and easy to read?

Once you start putting yourself in the reader's shoes you will begin to see why these things are upsetting to them.

Communication

Whether you are writing a cover letter or resume or having an in-person interview, you are communicating your messages to the potential employer.

The written message on its own becomes extremely important but it is the smallest part of the entire communications process and needs to be done well.

The Three Parts of Effective Communication

1. **Content:** The words you use - is responsible for only 7%
2. **Voice tones** and delivery – make up an additional 38%
3. **Body language** – is the largest at 55%

The above percentages represent the effectiveness of each in good communication. Each part has its role to play if you are to obtain optimum results.

All three happen

When you are successful in the entire hiring process

1)Written Content - or the spoken word content makes up only 7% of the communication process. This occurs when you present a cover letter, resume or references. It uses 7% of your ability to communicate. That is why your resume or cover letter must be the best you can make it.

a) Bad format or content could mean achieving only 1 or 2% of the 7% possible.

b) Mediocre format or content could accomplish 4% of the 7% available.

c) Exceptionally well-presented format or written content might attain 6 or 7% - or full potential.

2)Voice Tones and Delivery – make up 38% of your effective communication and will occur if you call or you are called on the phone for an interview, or when you are having one in person.

The following examples are mistakes people often make.

Examples

1. Speaking too fast.

     a. Hearing someone is not the same as understanding them.

     b. One needs to slow down to be understood.

2. Not pausing between thoughts or comments.

     a. Pausing provides time to let your message sink in.

3. Speaking in higher voice levels or voice tones.

     a. A high pitch voice is annoying.

     b. A lower pitched voice level creates trust and shows authority.

     c. Practice using lower voice tones.

4. Be enthusiastic and use different voice levels for emphasis.

     a. Speaking in a monotone will bore anyone and cause them to stop listening.

5. Trying to say too much on the telephone.

     a. Same some for the in-person interview

Body Language – makes up 55% and is the largest part of effective communication. Here, you use can either enhance your chances or end them.

If you are producing the body language, you do not want to do things that annoy your potential employer. You need to create trust and interest.

Being able to read other person's body language can tell you how well you are doing in your interview.

Note: We cover these areas of communication in detail in part 4 of our Sales Training Manual. – Called *"Meetings and Presentations"*

What levels of Communication

Do you wish to Achieve?

COVER LETTER AND RESUME HEADER

In our descriptions relating to the design preparation of your documents, we use Microsoft word 365 as our basis for our instructions as it would become too confusing for the reader, if we should try to cover others as well.

Page Margins

This will be the first part of the construction of your page that will act as your standard letterhead when applying for positions.

It is here that you will set the boundaries for your base document.

- For an 8.5 X 11-inch page go to Layout and click margins

- Use normal margins – one inch or 2.54 cm is good **(all 4 sides)**

- A narrow margin – usually ½ inch or 1.27 cm, is also acceptable. Make sure everything is still in your print zone.

Header, Footer Page Numbers

This is the second part of the construction of your page layout and it will contain your name, address, telephone number, and/or email address.

Click on Insert at the top left of your word document. After doing this, you will see the words – Header, Footer and Page Number appear approximately 2/3 of the way across the top, to your right.

Click on Header and look for the type you want. You will see some examples of the main types you can use - or choose search for more.

Click on your choice. - You can edit your choice or remove it if you wish. Once you have made your choice the *Header Footer Page Number* heading will move to the left side of your word document bar,

Click *"Home"* and your tools will appear in their original spot.

Under Design there will be some choices

a) Different front page – Leave this blank.

b) Different odd and even – When you check this – It removes header from page 2.

   a. You can choose to leave the header at top of page 2 by not checking it.

c) Show document text – check this – to be able to see any text below the header while there.

For Your Header Font Size

Type your name at top of header in Times Roman 14 font – no larger than 16.

Examples compared to page text of 12 font

- John Doe – 14 font
- John Doe – 16 font
- JOHN DOE 14 font
- **JOHN DOE** All caps and in 16 Bold?

- Click – Space bar to go to next line below the name
- Under your name, you will now start the line for your address.
- In 8 or 9 fonts, type in your address, telephone number and email address.
- Leave horizontal space between address telephone number and email address.
- For address line, you can start to the right or center it – whichever looks best to you?
- To create space below this line use space bar or "see our section on final spacing.

Two Header Examples

John Doe

24 Evergreen Drive, Orangeville Ontario A1A 2B2   -   Tel. (111) 234 - 2468   -   Email – jdoe@gmail.com

JOHN DOE

24 Evergreen Drive, Orangeville Ontario A1A 2B2   -   Tel. (111) 234 - 2468   -   Email – jdoe@gmail.com

Once Header is Done

1. Click – Save- Keep this as your base letterhead for everything.
2. **To Close Header** - find the red box with an X (usually far right) – You click this when you are finished and want to leave your header and go back to main page.
3. To re-enter Header – double click inside the Header space
4. Finally, if you are not happy you can remove it and start the process all over.

SUMMARY OF LETTERHEAD

You have now completed your base letterhead for all your cover letters and resumes. You will keep this as your base.

 Start each new document off by "save as" and then name the new document.

CONTENT FORMATTING

Document Formatting

Content Font and Size

- Use - Normal Style
- Times Roman is most common
- 12 font size is standard

Headings and Titles

- Use 12 font sizes for basic content presentation.
- Main Headings & Titles use size 12 font - CAPITALIZED.
- Sub Headings can be lower case 12 font with first letter in caps **Example** - (Duties).
- Do not Increase font size for emphasis.
- Bold is optional for some headings, but it can become overwhelming
- Paragraphs should be 3 to 4 lines
- Point form should be 1 line to 2 lines maximum

Clarity

Keep messages to one per sentence for clarity. Shorter sentences can achieve this.

Emphasis

- No color for emphasis
- No bold in middle of sentences for emphasis
- No Italics for emphasis unless it is a quotation
- No Abbreviations unless required by repetition and provide full version with Abbreviation in brackets first.

Initial Spacing of your Content

Most default settings between paragraphs will be either 6pt or 8pt spaces. This will be the amount of space created by the space bar. *(See our section on "final spacing" to adjust when document is done)*.

Finish your complete resume or cover letter without creating extra spacing caused by clicking the spacing bar multiple times. Use the space bar once for normal spacing for a new sentence or paragraph.

Do not completely fill the two pages. You should leave some space at bottom of each page as you will want more space for section headings etc.

When you have completed your document, you will then need to make some desired areas stand out.

See our next chapter on FINAL SPACING ADJUSTMENT

FINAL SPACING ADJUSTMENTS

When all the content for your documents is done, it will be the right time to adjust your spacing.

The following paragraphs will contain a description of how to create a more infinite control of spacing. It is an alternative to just using the enter or space bar. It will allow better use of the limited space that you have for your cover letter or resume.

We have included this spacing control description for those who wish to take it one step further than the normal method of spacer bar. The choice is ultimately up to you – space bar or spacing control (Layout).

The first thing you will need to do is find out where you have used the spacing bar to create extra space already

To Discover Extra Spaces Created by "the Bar"

Look at the top of your word document page; while in the **"Home"** position. Just below your main tool bar about half way across, you will find a symbol that looks like a backwards facing P with the top of the P filled in.

Right after this reversed P, is a line that looks sort of like a Capital T. It is joined to the top of the reversed P on the right side of the reversed P.

Click this symbol or box and it will now appear at the end of each paragraph or list that you have already created with the spacing bar. Click it again and they all disappear.

Unwanted Extra Space

When this symbol is activated, you will see the symbol at the end of each paragraph. This symbol will also appear where you have created extra space between paragraphs or items in a list.

Where one or more symbols appear between items in a list or between paragraphs, delete each of these symbols. The ones at the end of each list or paragraph are OK.

After you have removed the extra spaces created by the "Enter Bar", click the symbol at the top again to remove them from your page, and you will have a crowded but clean looking page to work with.

How to Create Extra Space the best way

Spacing After Page Header

We finished creating your header by suggesting there was another way to leave extra space below while in the header section.

1. Double click your Header and you are in.

2. In your top toolbar when at the home setting, **Click Layout** - go across to the Spacing heading in the area just below.

3. You will see two boxes Before and After. Before refers to the space above the line or before it. After is the space after the line or below it.

4. Place your curser at the end of the line where you want to create the extra space above or below.

5. In the header position leave the "Before" box at 0.

6. In the "After" Box - Click on the arrows up or down to create your desired spacing between your page title and the address line below.

7. Do the same for additional space below the address line.

8. To Exit your Header section - Double click your main page.

Overall Document Setting

We will now look at your main document content. Once your document is finished and extra space from space bar has been removed; we need to start with a uniform looking page.

Highlight everything in the main body of your document below the header as if you were going to cut or copy it.

Note: Your header is not included in this highlighting procedure.

The following process will enable you to create uniform spacing for all the content in the body of your whole document to get started.

With Everything now highlighted

- ✓ In your toolbar, **Click Layout**
- ✓ Go across to Paragraph and Spacing.
- ✓ Leave "Before" at 0 pts.
- ✓ Whatever is specified in "After"- Click on 6pt to start
- ✓ Click to remove the highlighting of your document(s).
- ✓ You now have a uniform space between lists and paragraphs.
- ✓ You can now adjust spaces between lines, paragraphs and headings on an individual basis.

Your Individual Spacing Control

After making the spacing uniform in your overall document

- o Place your cursor at the end of your last point in any sentence or a list or paragraph, or the heading where you want to create more space after (below) it.
- o Left click to position yourself in that location. Then go to the page layout. Locate the *"After Box"* in spacing.
- o You can increase the space after the cursor position in your document by left clicking the UP arrow until you have obtained the space desired. (8, 10, 12, or more).
- o Do this for each heading or paragraph where you want to increase the space after, remembering to keep things consistent.
- o Point setting before works on the same principal and is used only in certain situations like at the top of a page – before a heading. *Most Often - Leave before blank or 0.*
- o It is important to keep spacing consistent after each item in a list or at the end of paragraphs for overall appearance.
- o If you fail to be consistent and have some headings set 6 points after, similar headings set at 12 or 18 after, the document will look choppy and will be upsetting to the eye.
- o We suggest leaving all your "point-form" lists at 6 points to start (keep them all the same)
- o Experiment with point form spacing once you are finished the entire document, for best results.

Suggested Settings in Resume

Our resume document starts with the heading OVERVIEW.

1. To create space below your header and above the word OVERVIEW, we use the "Before" spacing box. **(One of the few places before is used)**

2. Set "Before" OVERVIEW at 22pt to 30pt to start.

3. For the space below OVERVIEW, we use the "After" box. It could be set at 14pt to 18pt by placing the curser at the end.

   - Do the same 22 – 30 for page 2 if you keep the Header.

   - If Page 2 has no header you can set the "Before" spacing to suit desired appearance for space at the top. (do not crowd)

Other Areas

- Items in a list – leave at 6

- Between several paragraphs in a row, 8 - 12 is good.

- After a paragraph before a Heading could be 14 – 18 pt. (using after box)

- After a sub heading, could be 8 to 12pt. spacing. (using after box)

Default Settings

You initially have set all spacing for 6pt after and everything will remain positioned here until they are individually changed physically by you.

You can change the space after items in a list, by highlighting the entire list and clicking the arrow in the after box up or down to your desired setting.

- Keep all lists the same, if you alter their original setting.

- After the last point in a list could be set at 12 to 18 for appearance.

Adjust your space settings to suit total content and appearance

Experiment and become familiar with the process

"BE CONSISTENT"

Experiment with the different settings until you are familiar with all the controls you have for appearance. It will take some time and effort to get it right.

General Tips

1. Less content allows more use of space for emphasis
2. A lot of content will risk becoming overcrowded and hard to read
3. It is better to reduce content than eliminate space
4. Adjust your spacing to suit total content
5. Be consistent in your spacing below titles, between sections and sentences

Use the other components in the normal section at top of word - for bullets, numbering, indenting, line positioning as well as your tab spacing bar. All your positioning and spacing controls are there.

These are your tools to create a document that someone will want to read.

Get familiar with all of them. A well-presented document will save a lot of time searching in the long run. Your documents will get more attention and many more readings, and more interviews as well.

Note: If the above instructions for space control seems too complicated – just use the enter bar for spacing. It is not as effective for best spacing control – but it works.

Note: – Spacing gives the reader room to breathe and for you to be able to increases the clarity of your message. It reduces the impression of too difficult to read.

LESS WRITTEN IS OFTEN MORE SAID

COVER LETTER

COMPONENTS

Part One - Page Header

- Your name, address, telephone number and email address at top.

Part Two – The Employers Company Information

a. Their company full name – top left main letter body
b. Their full address, below company name (see resume samples)
c. Telephone number below the address
d. Email address is optional beside the telephone # (both are handy for your own follow up)

Part Three – Date below address

- Month / Day / Year
  - March 12, 2016

Part Four – Attention - to whom it is written and title

- Left side below date
- Attention: **Bill Smith**
- Provide correct title – **Sales Manager**

Example

Attention: Bill Smith

       Sales Manager

Part Five – Dear Sirs/Madam

Part Six – Opening Statement

You must open with a statement that has impact.

- You must say something that will catch their attention right away to get them to read further.

- One or two paragraphs of 3 to 4 lines maximum

- You can have 3 Paragraphs **ONLY** if they are shorter, all meaningful and have Impact

- One mediocre paragraph of 7 or 8 lines will mean loss of effectiveness of your opening statement

Part Seven – Their Wants – You Offer

- This should be in point form

- Two columns

Examples

You Require		I Offer
Degree in Marketing	-	Graduated University of Fakeville
Project Management	-	Have managed over twenty-five (25) projects
Sales Experience	-	Have four years' Sales Experience

Part Eight – Ending

Finish on a positive or high note.

You say: *"I look forward to having the opportunity to discuss what benefits I have to offer your company and I will follow up to see when we can talk."*

Part Nine - The Signature

Yours truly,

SIGNATURE

Bill Smith

Note: The next page is a Sample COVER LETTER

Using Spacing and Font Sizing

John Doe

24 Evergreen Drive, Fakeville, Ontario A1A 2A2   Tel. (111) 234 - 2468   Email jdoe@lmail.com

THE HAPPY SAVER

222 North Street,

Sunnyville, Ontario L1L 2J2

Tel. 111-555-9076   email jsmith@lmail.com

Date: March 12, 2016

Attention: John Smith

              President

Dear Sir;

Ability is what you can do. Motivation determines what you do. Attitude determines how well you do it. – Lou Holtz

Enthusiasm, positive thinking, a desire to learn and a willingness to work hard, is what I offer.

The Corner Print Shop position gave me exposure to creating advertising for local businesses as well as selling our services to them. I believe I would be a great asset and the right candidate to provide sales for your company.

You Require	I Offer
Sales experience	Three Part time retail sales jobs including two years with "The Corner Print Shop"
Sales skills	I completed three sales training Courses: WES Marketing, Dale Carnegie, Brian Tracey
Transportation	My own vehicle which is new and reliable

I have the ability and am well motivated and believe that by granting me an interview, you will see why I am a suitable choice for this sales position.

Yours truly,

Signature

John Doe

RESUME

COMPONENTS

We suggest typing all your headings in Caps 12 Font (Times New Roman) and to center them on the document page.

Check our sample of a resume to see what it should look like. The following headings below are part of our *Table of Contents* formatting and should not be confused with your document formatting.

A - Overview

- This is the first category of the resume body under the header.
- Type OVERVIEW in Caps, center it and then ***bold it*** if you wish.
- Below OVERVIEW you will start with your opening remarks.

Note: you could call OVERVIEW something else like INTRODUCTION or PREVIEW. I just prefer Overview.

You must now open with a statement that has "impact"

What I mean by **"impact"** is that you must say something that will catch the reader's attention right away to get them to read further. One paragraph 2 to 4 lines is optimum.

Example impact statement on its own

OVERVIEW

In my present job I achieved the top sales position within the first nine months reaching $6,200,000 in sales. In the first year, I out-sold the combined volumes of the six other sales representatives in the company and continue to do so.

Adding more

You could add 1 or 2 more paragraphs **"ONLY"** if they are meaningful and have the same Impact as your opening statement.

The danger of 1 or 2 additional paragraphs could mean loss of impact of your opening statement.

An example of adding a BAD second paragraph after the above opening statement

"In public school I had a paper route and increased my circulation from 12 to 96 in the first six months."

B – Skills Offered

Option One of SKILLS OFFERED – Open Style

Use short form with 1 to 3 words per skill set with 3 to 4 per line without crowding. Use centering controls for lines to center each line. Keep distances between each skill the same.

SKILLS OFFERED

Marketing Plan Creation   Marketing Plan Implementation

Advertising   Prospecting   Sales Presentations

Closing the Sale   Answering Objections

Provide 6 to 9 skill offered in total. Again, do not repeat skills or crowd the lines as they are to stand out and should not fill the section.

Option Two of SKILLS OFFERED – Two groups

You can split the page into two groups if your skills offered descriptions are longer and center it on the page.

Center each line and keep spacing between skills the same.

SKILLS OFFERED

Proficient at Creating Sales Plans   Skilled at Prospecting

Excellent Closing Skills   Results Oriented

2 - Option Three – SKILLS OFFERED – Group List Style

It can be used in addition **OR** to replace either version of Options one or two. It is your choice if available space allows. Headings will change with job requirements.

If you are using two of these options in your resume, DO NOT repeat the same skills in each as it is a waste of space and might appear to be just fluff or filler.

Examples - Each of Featured Skill titles could contain 1 to 3 examples in point form. In this case you will not center the lines but have them start to the far-left side. Bold the headings and list 2 or 3 items per heading.

SKILLS OFFERED

Technical Capabilities

- Experienced in Photo-Shop
- Experienced in Design Concept and Auto-Cad

Business Management

- Organized and hosted our company's monthly webinar series
- Organized and chaired our company's monthly sales meetings

Sales and New Account Development

- Doubled previous annual sales in the first 11 months of employment
- Increased the average sale by 26%
- Increased customers by 34%

C – Relevant Experience

- This is optional and a good substitute when a Job History is limited or none existing.

- If you have experience that is not in the form of a job, place it under this heading.

- It could be projects you have done while in school or for any of the organizations you belong to. – This can be used along with job history.

D– Job History - Content to Use

We have already disused how to handle little or no job history. When it comes to job history and your experience one thing is certain.

The more history you have and the more experience you have gained – the more selective becomes the task of what you put in this part of your resume.

The most important area of your job history will be the most recent job(s) or the last five to seven years – go back10 years' tops.

Leave out jobs where your stay was less than 5 to 7 months unless it is your present job, or you are just starting out. That is why we show years only in our length of stay – not month and year

(Shown in PART E (2) of this section)

Job Before Existing

If the work history before your most recent job is more important for the job application in question; explain it in your cover letter and expand on it as needed in your resume.

You should also explain in either cover letter or in your resume (where space is available). Say why you wish to return to this area and why your recent experience increases your value to fulfill the undertakings of their advertised position (if you can).

Promotions within a Company

Perhaps your length of stay has been longer than four to seven years and you have moved up in seniority during this time while in the same company. Consider breaking your job experience for this company into sections to reflect these changes of duties and results.

It is good to show promotions within a company.

Separating position types to show this advancement can be a very effective way to highlight this fact, especially if your stay there has been lengthy. It shows both personal and job growth.

When outlining your experience, always show how your knowledge will benefit the potential new employer.

It is difficult to keep your resume from going over 2 pages if you try to list more than three jobs in detail with extensive lists of duties and accomplishments. Always give the most attention to the part of your job history that matches the job type you are applying for.

Larger Resumes

<u>Note</u>: In cases where a more detailed job history is required for a senior position there will be a totally different format for these called *"curriculum vitae"*. Here the number of pages could reach 10 or more.

We will not cover that scenario in this book.

It is not uncommon; however, for this senior position process to also start with a two-page resume and one-page cover letter.

The trend today is still the need for focused information to make narrowing the selection process quicker and easier for the employer.

E- Job History – The Design Format

E (1) Company Information

Put these points in one or two lines

- Company name
- Where it was located
- What its products or services were
- Put Contact Names, Address and Telephone Number in your references not here.
- If you list a job in Job History, you should provide the names and contact information in your references. Do not omit them.
- Add *See Reference package for contact information

Examples:

ABC Company – Toronto Ontario, Canada

Manufacturer and Supplier of Paint and Wood Finishes

Or

Coatings Application Company Limited

Toronto Ontario, Canada

Design, Building and Installation of Painting Systems

E (2) – Job Title and Time Employed

- Your Position or Title
  - General Manager
- Years you were there
  - Use the year only 2002 to 2004
  - **NOT** Months and year - April 2002 to March 2004

Examples:

General Manager – 2002 to 2004

Sales Representative – 2002 to 2004

Assistant Marketing Manager – 2002 to 2004

E (3) – Duties

Duties examples

1. Create and Implement Sales Plans
2. Responsible for all Sales for the company

Do these sections indented or in your choice of point form (numbers here are very good) and relate your duties and your accomplishments to the skill sets you have shown above.

Keep Duties to max of 3 lines unless you have only one or two jobs in your history and need to expand.

E (4) – Accomplishments

Accomplishments examples

1. Reduced Advertising costs by 29% through analytics
2. Increased Sales by 285% - over 2 years

Do these sections also in point form (again numbering your point form can be more effective. Be consistent for both duties and accomplishments.

Relate your accomplishments to the skill sets stated at the start. Keep Accomplishments to two lines unless you have only one or two jobs in your history and need to show more accomplishments.

Other special accomplishments can also be shown later

(If there is room)

Under the heading – "OTHER ACCOMPLISHMENTS"

When you are providing the descriptions of duties and accomplishments have the main duties or best accomplishments for each job. Do not try to list everything you did at each place of employment.

Avoid saying the same things twice for your different jobs listed.

"Experience"

"You can have five years of diverse experience

Or you can repeat one years' experience five times"

Make sure your experience does not look like the same things over and over without any growth or advancement of new knowledge or abilities. Do not repeat similar experiences or accomplishments.

F – Education

- Name the university or institution and where it was located
- Provide contact information here or say see reference package
- Name the course that you took and time period
- Explain what it covered in point form in one line (Optional – more, if you have enough room)
- State that you graduated - if you did and when
- If you have letters - Such as P Eng. - Use them everywhere you can.

G – Professional Courses

- Name any further education especially if related to the job type
- Explain what they were and when you took them
- Say where they were. Say you completed them (if you did)

H - Interests and Professional Memberships

- List any special interest or hobbies that are relevant to the job application
- List any professional groups or organizations that you belong to
- Name any charitable organizations you belong to
- Join associations if you are not in any - Like *"Chamber of Commerce."* and list them
- List volunteer groups you have joined

I – Social Networking

- List any online networking groups like *Face Book or LinkedIn*
- Show your number of contacts if they are significant
- List online discussion groups relating to your job. *LinkedIn* has many for sales and marketing

Today social networking and contacts are a very big part of sales and marketing. This section will demonstrate how far your reach is in your online activities.

J – Other Accomplishments

Optional - If you have any special accomplishments not mentioned elsewhere and you feel they are important, list them here. It might be the fact that you have designed and managed web-sites.

Summary

This will complete the main parts of your resume. Keep your completed resume to two pages' maximum. While cover letters are very specific, resumes can often have a wider reach.

When targeting different industries where you have experience make sure you change the content to suit the type of industry you are focusing on or applying to.

Note: The following two pages contain the Sample Resume.

Normally the Minimum Font size you should use on a normal sized page of 8.5 inches by 11 inches would be size 12.

To fit our Sample Resume on two 6-inch x 9-inch pages; which is the size of this book, we had to reduce the font to 11.

In this way, we can demonstrate how the overall appearance should be.

As we say Appearance is everything.

John Doe

24 Evergreen Drive, Fakeville, Ontario A1A 2A2   Tel. (111) 234 - 2468   Email – jdoe@lmail.com

OVERVIEW

I make things happen and possess all the requirements that you are asking for in a Sales Representative and have demonstrated my ability to achieve results.

SKILLS OFFERED

Experience in Advertising   Prospecting   Making Presentations

Closing the Sale   Answering Objections   Self Starter   Results Oriented

WORK EXPERIENCE

See Reference Package for Contact Information

THE CORNER PRINT SHOP   Fakeville Ontario   Printing Services

Sales Clerk 2011 to 2014 – Part Time

DUTIES

1. Make Prospecting telephone calls and in person visits to local businesses
2. Order desk, counter service, cash register and shop equipment cleaning

ACCOMPLISHMENTS

1. Established 32 new customers over the 2 years of part time employment
2. Achieved 27% of the total sales working part time and in the summer.

BILLS HARDWARE Fakeville Ontario   Retail outlet hardware supplies

Sales Clerk 2010- 2011 – Part time

DUTIES

1. Selling gift items, sports products, servicing customer needs for home repair. Cleaning the store and setting up displays

ACCOMPLISHMENTS

1. Established a program to supply local schools with sporting equipment that increased annual sales by 195%

DISCOUNT SHOES Fakeville, Ontario   Retail Outlet Footwear

Sales Clerk – 2009 to 2010 – Part Time

DUTIES

1. Sales Clerk – looked after all sales needs
2. Store duties included stocking shelves and cash register

ACCOMPLISHEMENTS

1. Received highest in sales award for the part time sales help team of five part-time employees.

EDUCATION

Fakeville High School – 2009 to 2012 Graduated with Honors

PROFESSIONAL COURSES

Dale Carnegie - Public Speaking

Direct Sales Academy 101 – Five Part Sales Training Course

INTERESTS AND PROFESSIONAL MEMBERSHIPS

Member of the Fakeville Chamber of Commerce

Member of Fakeville drama Club

SOCIAL ONLINE GROUPS

FACEBOOK – 1,760 Contacts and Friends

LINKEDIN – 1,472 Contacts

Twitter – 2,845 – Followers

OTHER ACCOMPLISHEMENTS

School President – Fakeville High School 2011/2012

Public Speaking - First Place 2012 Ontario high school competition

Athlete of the year - Fakeville High School – 2009/10 and 2010/11

COVER LETTERS AND RESUMES

You have taken the time to create the best resume and cover letter that you possibly can so why stop there. It is often the person who goes a little bit further than the rest that wins the prize or gets the job.

The Presentation

Why just hand in a resume paper clipped or stapled together or in an envelope or stuffed loosely in a folder, when you can create impact with how you present everything.

Start with a cover page that is specifically made for the company and/or job in question.

Some Design Tips for Cover

- Center it on the page
- Use business colors for print – black, dark gray or darker shades of blue
- Bold or Normal depending on color chosen and appearance
- Use page color that is business acceptable white, light grey or light gray/blue
- NO REDS or Bright colors for print or pages
- You can make it a heavier bond than your resume and something with a Quality appearance and feel to it.
- Staple your presentation cover, cover letter and resume together and put a triangular corner cover in the top left corner over the staple.

Other ideas

- You can purchase a folder with pockets. Make sure you label it with your name and "attention of" and place your documents inside.
- Or perhaps better - three hole punch your documents and place them in a folder with a clear front cover.

- It is too easy to get lost if front cover is not a *"See **through**"*
- Be creative but do not overkill as it is a business presentation.

RESUME AND COVER LETTER

For

JOHN SMITH – PRESIDENT

Of

FAKE BUSINESS

For the Position of

SALES REPRESENTATIVE

ABOVE IS A SAMPLE COVER

THE REFERENCE PACKAGE

REFERENCE SELECTION

Part 1 will be your Cover Page for your reference Package.

Part 2 of your Reference package will be your Reference cover letter to match the resume you are using and provide a little introduction discussing briefly why you used the references chosen.

- **Note:** We have indicated that you should state *"See reference Package for Contact information"* in the job history section, so make sure that references are provided for every job shown in your Job History.

Part 3 – Is your Reference Information. It could be one or more pages and should list who the references are and all their contact information.

- Add any appropriate documents or letters they might have written.

- You should provide Contact names, addresses and telephone numbers for any companies or organizations shown in your job history.

- Additional references should be selected for the type of company you are applying to as well.

- Include Education contact information and telephone numbers if they are important to your qualifications and not in your resume.

References should be accurate

Do not randomly hand out references if they are not relevant to the position you are applying for unless they are personal references. If it is a personal reference and is not job related - say so and why you have provided it.

Matching references to the job applied for shows organizational skills. Most of all, it shows respect for the potential employer's time and information required to reach a decision.

The employer will become annoyed if you appear to suggest anything will do as a reference. This will indicate that you do not need to provide accurate and suitable proof of your experience, skill sets or character traits.

Inform Your References

"Most of all" - Make sure that the person(s) you use as a reference know(s) that you are planning to use them and what you have said.

Give them a copy of the cover letter, resume and reference page that you have used. Show them what you have said about yourself and the referenced person.

Provide this information

To each person used as a reference.

This will provide a comfort zone for all your references.

There is nothing worse than a surprised person on the other end of the phone who is totally unprepared for the employers call and what they should say about you.

Out of respect for all parties and to obtain the best reference possible as well.

Do it right!

For most of job types, you will usually be expected to provide at least three job related references. Some may not request references until your interview, but we suggest providing them with your cover letter and resume as a separate document.

This creates continuity and makes the employers follow through easier.

There is a professional format for presenting references and the more professional the position, the more professional you should look.

Keep the cover letter and resume separate from the references but probably in the same folder if that is your overall presentation package

Usually all references will be contacted so use your best ones for the job you have applied to. By letting your references know what you are saying about them and yourself, they will be totally prepared.

Some questions could go beyond the scope of the submitted documents. By having a copy of what you have provided to the potential employers, your references will be able to give much better responses. They will also be more willing to support your efforts.

When References are requested

The Timing for Requesting References will vary.

- We feel they should be presented with the resume and cover letter. But keep the two areas separate with each having their own cover page.

- They are part of the total package of YOU that is being presented so why leave them out.

- If sent by email use PDF to keep things formatted properly which also applies to your cover letter/resume package.

- If emailing is requested a hard copy should be provided when you have your interview.

Reference Package Design Criteria

- Use the same design options as Cover letter and Resume
- You will have three sections
  - o Cover page
  - o Cover Letter
  - o Contact and Reference Information- 1 or more pages
- Again, be creative but do not go overboard.

Reference Sample Part 1 – Cover is on the next Page

John Doe

24 Evergreen Drive, Fakeville Ontario A1A 2A2 - Tel. (111) 234 - 2468 - Email – jdoe@lmail.com

REFERENCES

Provided for

JOHN SMITH – PRESIDENT

Of

FAKE BUSINESS

For the Position of

SALES REPRESENTATIVE

John Doe

24 Evergreen Drive, Fakeville Ontario A1A 2A2   -   Tel. (111) 234 - 2468   -   Email – jdoe@lmail.com

FAKE BUSINESS LIMITED

Address,

Telephone number, email (if available)

Date

Attention: JOHN SMITH

       PRESIDENT

Dear Sirs;

I have selected the following testimonials and character references for your viewing and you may contact them whenever desired.

I have chosen these people as they best represent my experience in the type of position that you are advertising. I also have supplied a character reference as well from someone in my community.

The people used as a reference have copies of my resume and cover letter that I have provided to you. Feel free to ask any questions that you deem relevant and important for consideration of my employment.

I look forward to meeting with you and will follow up in one week if I have not heard from you to see when we can get together.

Yours truly,

Signature

John Doe

John Doe

24 Evergreen Drive, Fakeville Ontario A1A 2A2   -   Tel. (111) 234 - 2468   -   Email – jdoe@lmail.com

Support Documents Submitted (state # of pages)

A) Personal References letters (Attach any letters)

1. Name, telephone number and relationship
2. Name, telephone number and relationship

B) Job references for Telephone follow up (list below)

(Sample 1 Job reference to call)

- o Name
- o Position, Company and relationship
- o Business number 111-222-3456
- o Home number 222 333 8765 (get permission)

(Sample Job 2 reference to call)

- o Name
- o Position, Company and relationship
- o Business number 111-222-3456
- o Home number 222 333 8765 (get permission)

(Sample Job 3 reference to call)

   Same information as above if 3 are supplied)

C) Copies of Diplomas and Awards (Attach copies)

- Academic Certificates – provide a list and attach copies
- Training Certificates – provide a list and attach copies
- Awards – provide a list and attach copies
- Include names and contact information for all documents in C

Note: Number pages in part 3 – show as 1 of 5, 2 of 5 until the total is reached.

THE INTERVIEW

WHAT TO CONSIDER

Make a List

1. Make a list of things you feel are important to discuss in your interview.
2. Bring extra copies of your cover letter, resume and references.
3. Bring copies of any other documentation like sales training certificates.

Personal Hygiene

Shower, wash your hair, clean your fingernails, and brush your teeth. Shave if it is relevant. Comb, brush or style your hair whichever is applicable.

Wear suitable deodorant and use a mouth wash if you might suspect bad breath. Breath mints are acceptable but - "Do Not Chew Gum."

Appearance

Dress for the occasion. Do not dress too casually even for a position in a casual working environment. Wear clothes that are freshly washed, ironed or have been dry-cleaned. Perhaps check out the companies dress codes before you show up for the interview.

To dress in formal attire shows respect and it is not usually a problem. Dressing too casually will set you off on the wrong foot immediately.

Make sure your clothes match. Polish your shoes if they can be polished. Make sure any accessories are not over the top. Wear an acceptable level of makeup if it is appropriate.

Show Up on Time

It is best to show up a few minutes in advance. Five minutes ahead is best, and a maximum of 10 minutes ahead is acceptable.

More is not acceptable as it may disrupt the interviewer's schedule and possibly anger them to try and accommodate an early arrival.

Wait outside or somewhere close (if required)

To arrive at the right time

Being late is Terminal

If you feel you will be even 2 - 5 minutes late, it better be a very good reason. All you can do is call and explain your situation and apologize for any inconvenience.

Make sure your new arrival time is acceptable to them and even offer to re-schedule another day if it is going to be more than 10 minutes behind the preset time.

Being late is not good and will create a very bad first impression regardless of the reason. Being Late for an appointment when you are employed and seeing prospects will not be what your potential employer wants to see.

Do it here and they will suspect the worst if you are hired.

Do not Create a Double Negative Impression

When stating your new expected arrival time, be accurate and allow a little extra time for your revised appointment time. Do not say you will be 10 minutes late if you already know it will be 15 or 20.

The Best Arrival Time of course is – On-Time

Personal Traits

Be Courteous, Respectful and Likable.

The way you introduce yourself and behave in your interview is how your potential employer will see you greeting their customers. Their impression will be what the customer's first impression will be.

The three attributes to be *"Courteous, Respectful and Likable"* will go a long way in the consideration of who gets the position. If one of these elements is missing you have reduced your chances by a considerable amount.

Show Enthusiasm

Enthusiasm will provide excitement and confidence and will often turn the decision in the direction of the person who shows the most of it unless they go overboard.

Enthusiasm in a genuine form is contagious; and when a customer catches it, they will usually buy.

Key Points

Mention the Key points of your Resume.

Even though the interviewer may have your resume in front of them, do not assume they remember everything in it. If it is a key point and they have missed it - **Say** *"As you may recall in my resume"* - mention the key points.

Clubs or Organizations

Selling is all about outgoing people who connect with others. Mention if you are or have been in public speaking, a drama club, Chamber of Commerce or are now part of any extra curricula activity. These things demonstrate qualities that are important in sales.

If you know the main benefits of their product or services over the competition and can briefly talk intelligently about those subjects; you have already surpassed most of the people applying, who have not taken this initiative.

Do not over do this part either as it will also backfire!

Sales Training

If you have shown in your resume that you have taken sales training that contains the important elements required to do the job, talk about them. Show the interviewer any certificate(s) you may have. Provide photo copies or list them if you cannot show them original copies.

You have been given the opportunity of having this interview; it is now time to sell yourself with enthusiasm to get the position.

Most of all let your very own personality come out.

Do not be afraid of being yourself and letting them see who you really are. Always show respect and do not get too personal. Getting too familiar or flip will usually spell disaster.

Be friendly and be a likable person, because their customers will also need to see the real you and like that person as well. Remember they are hiring a person, not a knowledgeable robot. If they see and hire the real person, you will not work surrounded by pretense.

Be happy, be Positive, be Enthusiastic, and be Natural.

The employer will look for ways to narrow the field quickly, until they can reach the desired number of candidates that they will call back for a final interview.

Become one of the people who stand out in a positive way and cause them to put you into the right pile.

The Voice

Your Voice and how you use it makes up 38% of potential communication. This happens in the telephone follow up and interview. Choosing what to say and how you say it can make the difference in being considered or not.

Effective voice usage can range from an annoying 0 to 38% effective

- High squeaky voices are usually annoying and are very low on the effectiveness scale. (especially for sales)
- Just think of someone with a squeaky or shrill voice that you hate.
- Using your lower voice range creates more authority.
- Speaking in a monotone will soon put the listener to sleep.

Practice the lower voice range and changing voice levels for emphasis.

People tend to talk too fast when they are nervous.

- o Hearing someone is one thing but understanding what is said is another.

- o Speaking slowly with pauses in the right place implies you are thinking and it also gives both of you time to think.

- o By pausing you will not appear to be just rambling on.

- o Pausing also gives them time to understand the message you are presenting.

- o Practice speaking slower and pausing for effect.

- o Record your changes.

- o Listen to the differences.

- o Make the adjustments to make the proper presentation.

Silence and Pauses

Why do people fear the silence of a pause?

- In sales, the pause or silence after you have asked for the order is the most powerful tool that you can use to get the sale.

  - o The rule is – *"After you ask the closing question - SHUT UP! - SHUT UP AND LISTEN! - because the first person who speaks loses"*.

Speak slowly and use the pause

To allow your messages to sink in or get a response

When your Interview is over

Ask for the job

And then Shut Up and Listen

The Bad Words You Use

In our Sales book on Presentations we talk about the bad words people use when making their sales presentation. The same effort should be made here in your interview.

These same words will upset your potential employer and cause them to have second thoughts about you as a candidate for the job.

We will provide a few examples here. Avoid the use of words such as spiel, pitch contract, and sign to name a few. There are many others and they include slang as well as swearing or profanity.

Your choice of words will not only influence any prospect; it will also do the same here.

Body Language

Charles Darwin published his book in 1872 called *"The Expressions of the Emotions in Man and Animals"* and was the first to present these ideas.

In the 1960s, **Paul Ekman** a California psychiatrist, and an expert in facial expressions along with **Sorenson and Friesen** conducted and published the results of their extensive studies of a variety of peoples and cultures.

Their studies confirmed Darwin was right

Even though Body Language makes up 55% of our potential effectiveness in communicating skills, it is given the least consideration when we are making presentations.

Find out more about this subject as we have devoted a whole chapter to this subject in part 4 of our five-part Sales Training *"Meetings and Sales Presentations"*

Body language makes up the final part of your effective communication potential at 55%, and it happens during your interview.

It is here that using your body language effectively and being able to read other people's body language, can give you optimum control of any discussion or situation.

Many things can be very offensive in body language. The person who is unaware that certain things they do are upsetting to the listener, can quickly destroy their chances of being considered for the job.

The voice and your delivery are part of the final phase of being hired and it is here during your interview that you make your final impression in the hiring process.

Summary of the Interview

As we have shown, there are many parts to your Interview, and they are all important parts to the presentation of YOU. You must look at your interview as a final part of the recipe or formula to get the outcome you desire.

It is here that you will make or break your chances.

Study this section and related areas in our other books carefully as it will often be your final chance to be accepted for the position. Use good etiquette and good manners as they also play an important part in the consideration of you.

SUMMARY OF BOOK

Much of this book was written to help people that I was coaching understand where they were making their mistakes. I saw time and time again the same mistakes being made and heard the same stories of failure to get Interviews or to get hired.

The written word, the spoken word and the physical presentation of it are the three parts of achieving the results you are after.

The time taken to properly prepare your documents is never lost. Trying to achieve results with poorly formatted cover letters, resumes and references is like trying to win a race with weights fastened to your feet.

Quantity will never replace "Quality".

Sending large numbers of the same generic documents will almost always end in disappointment and will waste your time and money.

There is a lot of work in putting together professional looking documents that are crafted to meet the expectations of specific job types and environments.

Presenting yourself in the best possible way when arranging an interview and during your interview are the final parts of the hiring process.

By following the steps outlined in this book you will be creating a blueprint for success and will be on your way to *"Getting The Sales Job"*.

Wayne E Shillum – Author

www.ingramcontent.com/pod-product-compliance
Lightning Source LLC
Chambersburg PA
CBHW051416200326
41520CB00023B/7255